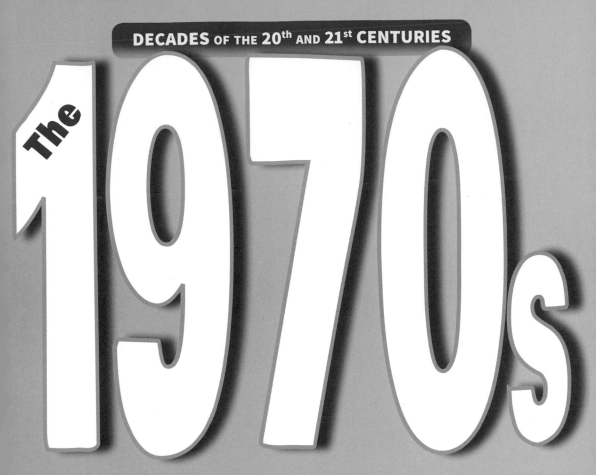

The 1970s

Stephen Feinstein

The 1970s

Stephen Feinstein

Enslow Publishing

101 W. 23rd Street
Suite 240
New York, NY 10011
USA

enslow.com

Published in 2016 by Enslow Publishing, LLC.
101 W. 23rd Street, Suite 240, New York, NY 10011

Library of Congress Cataloging-in-Publication Data

Feinstein, Stephen.
  The 1970s / Stephen Feinstein.
    pages cm. — (Decades of the 20th and 21st centuries)
  Includes bibliographical references and index.
  Summary: "Discusses the decade 1970-1979 in the United States in terms of culture, art, science, and politics"— Provided by publisher.
  Audience: Grade 9 to 12.
  ISBN 978-0-7660-6934-3
  1. United States—Civilization—1945- —Juvenile literature. 2. United States—Politics and government—1969-1974—Juvenile literature. 3. United States--Politics and government—1974-1977—Juvenile
literature. 4. United States—Politics and government—1977-1981—Juvenile literature. 5. Nineteen seventies—Juvenile literature. I. Title.
  E169.12.F4474 2015
  973.924—dc23

                    2015010949

Printed in the United States of America

To Our Readers: We have done our best to make sure all Web sites in this book were active and appropriate
when we went to press. However, the author and the publisher have no control over and assume no liability
for the material available on those Web sites or on any Web sites they may link to. Any comments or sugges-
tions can be sent by e-mail to customerservice@enslow.com.

Photo Credits: Alberto Roveri/Mondadori Portfolio via Getty Images, p. 67; Barbara Freeman/Hulton
Archive/Getty Images, p. 19; David Hume Kennerly/Hulton Archive/Getty Images, p. 64; David Hume
Kennerly/3rd Party - Misc/Getty Images, pp. 16, 89; David Redfern/Redferns/Getty Images, pp. 3 (top left),
28, 87 (top); Dennis Hallinan/Archive Photos/Getty Images, p. 86; Dirck Halstead/The LIFE Images Col-
lection/Getty Images, pp. 3 (bottom left), 80; Duane Howell/The Denver Post via Getty Images, p. 81; Ernst
Haas/Ernst Haas/Getty Images, pp. 15, 78; Fisherss/Shutterstock.com, p. 74; Focus on Sport/Getty Images,
pp. 3 (bottom right), 37, 38, 43, 88 (top); Hulton Archive/Archive Photos/Getty Images, pp. 3 (top right), 6;
Hulton Archive/Getty Images, p. 72; Jerry Cooke/Sports Illustrated/Getty Images, pp. 34, 40 87 (bottom);
John Dominis/The LIFE Picture Collection/Getty Images, p. 52; Julian Wasser/The LIFE Images Collection/
Getty Images, p. 82; Keystone-France/Gamma-Keystone via Getty Images, pp. 55, 60, 71; Keystone/Hulton
Archive/Getty Images, p. 51; Lambert/Archive Photos/Getty Images, p. 20; Michael Putland/Hulton Archive/
Getty Images, p. 31; Mondadori Portfolio via Getty Images, p. 10; NBC Television/Archive Photos/Getty
Images, p. 27; Reg Innell/Toronto Star via Getty Images, p. 76; Robee Shepherd/Moment/Getty Images, p. 77;
Roland Neveu/LightRocket via Getty Images, p. 45; Rolls Press/Popperfoto/Getty Images, p. 41; Ron Galella/
WireImage/Getty Images, p.12; Science & Socety Picture Library/ SSPL/Getty images, p. 59; Silver Screen
Collection/Moviepix/Getty Images, p. 25; Spencer Grant/Archive Photos/Getty Images, p. 46; STAFF/AFP/
Getty Images, p. 68; STRINGER/AFP/Getty Images, p. 48; Susan Wood/Hulton Archive/ Getty Images, p. 32;
Ted Dully/The Boston Globe via Getty Images, p. 63; Tom Munnecke/Hulton Archive/Getty Images, p. 75;
Universal History Archive/Universal Images group/Getty Images, pp. 56, 88 (bottom).

Cover Credits: David Redfern/Redferns/Getty Images (Jimi Hendrix); Dirck Halstead/The LIFE Images
Collection/Getty Images (Richard Nixon); Focus on Sport/Getty Images (Billie Jean King); Hulton Archive/
Archive Photos/Getty Images (soldiers).

Contents

The Vietnam War played a large part in America's "crisis of confidence."

Introduction

The 1970s were a time of struggle and doubt. For three decades, America had been a world leader. Its economy thrived, and its military was strong. By the 1970s, Americans began to sense a change. Suddenly, it seemed as if their country was losing its strength. President Jimmy Carter called it a "crisis of confidence."

The Vietnam War played a large role in the crisis. The war was different from past conflicts. US troops found it hard to tell friend from foe. The enemy struck quickly and then vanished. As the death toll grew, many people at home began to oppose the war. They staged protests, some of which led to bloodshed. College students were among the most vocal war protesters. By the mid-1970s, America had managed to get out of the war, but the deep divisions it had caused would take many years to heal.

Another conflict in the world caused many problems during the 1970s, which was the Arab-Israeli conflict. In 1948, Jewish people created the state of Israel in the Middle East. Arab nations there strongly opposed Israel. They fought several wars to destroy it but failed. Some Arab groups turned to terrorism and hijacked airplanes. In 1972, terrorists took hostages at the Olympics. America's support for Israel angered the Arab countries. In 1973, Arab countries decided to stop selling oil to the United States. The move triggered a US energy crisis. People ran short of gas for their cars and heating oil for their homes. America's economy was hit hard. Prices for food and other goods climbed. The government urged everyone to save fuel.

Americans were shocked to learn that President Richard Nixon had authorized a cover-up of his administration's involvement in the Watergate affair—an illegal break-in at the headquarters of the Democratic National Committee. The Watergate scandal ended Nixon's political career. He became the only president ever to resign from office. Like the Vietnam War, Watergate caused many people to distrust their government.

Bitter and exhausted, many Americans stopped getting involved in politics. They began to focus more on their own problems and needs. Young people who had become hippies in the 1960s looked for ways to rejoin the mainstream. They started to build careers and seek financial success. Writer Tom Wolfe noticed that Americans were becoming preoccupied with their own well-being. They were concerned with eating healthful foods and looking good. In 1976, Wolfe described the 1970s as the "Me Decade."

The 1970s saw some uplifting events, as well. An American swimmer named Mark Spitz made Olympic history. Slugger Hank Aaron broke baseball's long-standing record for career home runs. In 1976, America celebrated two hundred years of independence. However, more bad news would follow this celebration. In Jonestown, Guyana, more than nine hundred members of a religious cult took their own lives. An accident at a nuclear power plant in Pennsylvania nearly led to disaster. Such stories added to the sense of gloom many people felt during the 1970s.

As the decade ended, America seemed to reach a new low. Another energy crisis gripped the economy. In Iran, US embassy workers were being held hostage. The Soviet Union—America's Cold War rival—invaded Afghanistan. Nobody knew how these crises might end, and feelings of doubt ran stronger than ever.

Pop Culture, Lifestyles, and Fashion

Although the 1960s had been marked by upheaval—struggles for civil rights, the anti-Vietnam war movement, and urban rioting—that decade had been a period when many Americans enjoyed financial comfort.

Hippies Return to the Mainstream

Good economic conditions made it easy for young people to put off decisions about careers and marriage. Housing, food, and energy were cheap. A youth counterculture sprang up to protest any limits on personal freedoms. Young people felt free to question the traditional values of their parents, government, and religious leaders. The baby boom that took place after World War II created an enormous youth population. Four out of ten Americans in the mid-1960s were under the age of seventeen. It is no wonder they were able to cause such a stir. Members of the counterculture were often referred to as hippies. The main goal for many was to oppose the war in Vietnam. Others who were not so focused on politics also rejected traditional values. Sex, drugs, and rock 'n' roll were important elements of the hippie life-style. Hippies also experimented with communal living arrangements.

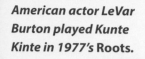

American actor LeVar Burton played Kunte Kinte in 1977's Roots.

Many men grew their hair long. The use of drugs, such as marijuana and LSD, increased dramatically. People became much more tolerant of sexual experimentation. It seemed to many that free love could become a part of everyday life. In the 1970s, the economy went through some drastic changes. Life became more difficult. Many people had trouble making ends meet. Dropping out of the main stream no longer seemed to be a wise option. Young people once again became concerned with making the right career decisions.

By the second half of the 1970s, however, it was clear that certain aspects of the youth counterculture had become part of mainstream culture. Rock 'n' roll had become a multibillion-dollar consumer business. It was now just as big a part of the American capitalist system as any other industry.

Black Is Beautiful

The civil rights movement led to a growing sense of ethnic pride among the various groups in the United States in the 1970s. African Americans focused on their African cultural heritage. They adopted African styles of fashion along with promoting awareness that black is beautiful. African American men wore their hair in natural Afro styles. African American women wore brightly colored, loose-fitting garments known as dashikis.

In 1977, a television miniseries based on Alex Haley's book *Roots* was broadcast. *Roots* told the story of Alex Haley's family history in America beginning with Kunta Kinte, who had been brought from Africa to work as a slave in Virginia in 1767. About 130 million Americans tuned in each night to follow the story of the succeeding generations of the Haley family.

Roots inspired pride in African Americans. But it also influenced members of other ethnic groups. All of a sudden, people seemed interested in learning about their own ethnic backgrounds. People

America Celebrates its Bicentennial

In 1976, the United States celebrated its bicentennial, or two-hundred-year anniversary, since declaring independence from Britain. The bicentennial celebration lasted for months.

People wore red, white, and blue clothing and flew the American flag. The US Mint issued special coins. The US Postal Service issued special stamps. A surge of patriotism swept across the country. People once again felt proud of their nation.

The revelry peaked on July 4, 1976. In Washington, D.C., President Gerald Ford led a huge celebration featuring fireworks and music. In New York harbor, a fleet of old-fashioned sailing ships gathered. People in Boston reenacted the Boston Tea Party.

Nearly every town and city in America held its own special celebration. There were picnics, fireworks, and parades. The bicentennial was an important cultural event. It brought the nation together during a difficult time.

joined ethnic political organizations and participated in ethnic neighborhood celebrations. Colleges and schools offered courses in ethnic studies. And with a little bit of research, it soon became apparent that all people, no matter what their ethnicity, had good reason to feel proud.

Hispanic Leaders

Millions of Hispanic Americans took pride in the heroic work of Cesar Chavez, the leader of the United Farm Workers Union. He used nonviolent tactics to gain better working conditions for farmworkers. He successfully organized sit-ins, picket lines, and consumer boycotts to win a bitter strike against California grape growers. In 1979, he led an eight-month strike against California lettuce growers.

Meanwhile, a Hispanic-American political group called La Raza Unida in East Los Angeles and the Southwest organized Hispanic-American workers to promote better working conditions and higher wages. And Spanish-language newspapers and Hispanic television stations also contributed to a growing sense of pride on the part of Hispanic Americans in their own culture.

American Indian Pride

American Indians, too, were inspired by the new sense of ethnic pride sweeping the nation. Their main concern was to protect their lands from further seizure by the federal or state governments. In 1972, about five hundred members of the American Indian Movement (AIM) seized the Bureau of Indian Affairs in Washington, D.C., to protest treaty violations. They occupied the building for a week. This action spurred the government to make changes at the bureau and begin to address the Indians' grievances.

In 1973, AIM protested unfair treatment of Indians by law officers at the Pine Ridge Reservation at Wounded Knee, South Dakota, which was the scene of a massacre of Indians by the United States Army in 1890. AIM's protests led to a two-month-long confrontation between Indians and police. The actions of AIM contributed to a growing sense of American Indian pride. The following year, Indians gained the right to control federal aid for education and other services on their reservations with the Indian Self-Determination Act of 1974.

American Indians continued to come under pressure from energy companies who wanted to drill for natural gas and mine coal and uranium on Indian lands. The courts granted Indians the right to negotiate their own contracts with energy companies. But in some places the activities of the energy companies disturbed the Indians' sacred burial grounds. Uranium mining and coal-burning power plants in particular caused environmental pollution on Indian lands. To protest such activities and draw attention to the situation, Indians in 1978 organized a peaceful demonstration called The Longest Walk. Indian activists walked three-thousand miles from San Francisco to Washington, D.C., a walk that took five months to complete.

In Search of Spiritual Guidance

The 1970s were a confusing time for many people. Those who had questioned traditional beliefs during the 1960s now needed to find something else in which to believe. Many were drawn to gurus, or spiritual guides, from India. Gurus were eager to train new disciples in various Indian religious or mystical traditions. Maharishi Mahesh Yogi became widely popular after the Beatles and other celebrities became followers. The Maharishi even appeared as a guest on Johnny Carson's *Tonight Show*.

Groups of people dressed in robes and chanting "Hare Krishna" became a common sight at airports and on busy downtown streets all

The American Indian Movement got people talking in the 1970s.

Nearly 1,000 Jonestown congregants committed mass suicide in 1978.

around the country. These people were followers of a guru known as Swami A. C. Bhaktivedanta.

People from many different religious traditions attracted groups of devoted followers. In some cases, cult members were brainwashed. The Reverend Sun Myung Moon, a South Korean Presbyterian minister, attracted a huge following of young people to his Unification Church. His followers came to be called Moonies.

The People's Temple cult came to a bizarre and tragic end in the 1970s. Founded in 1955 by Jim Jones, a Pentecostal minister, the religion was based on communist ideas, such as the equal sharing of property. Jones attracted many followers. In 1976, Jones relocated his one-thousand-person congregation to the jungles of Guyana and called it the Promised Land, which then became known as Jonestown. Isolated from the rest of the world, Jones began to preach to his followers that disaster was coming. In 1978, California Congressman Leo Ryan visited Jonestown to investigate conditions there at the request of families of cult members. As Ryan was leaving, he and several People's Temple members who were trying to leave Jonestown were murdered by Jones's followers. Fearing an attack by the US government, Jones directed more than nine hundred of his followers to drink poisoned Kool-Aid. Jim Jones shot himself in the head or was shot by an aide. Images of their dead bodies littering the ground startled the world.

Women Fight for Equality

Women were a major force for change in America in the 1970s. Throughout the decade, increasing numbers of feminists struggled for equal rights and an end to discrimination against women. They pressed for better educational opportunities, and as a result, Ivy League universities began to admit women as students. During the

1970s, there was a 500 percent increase in the number of women entering law schools. Forty percent of those entering medical schools were women, and 25 percent of doctorate degrees were earned by women.

Many types of jobs became available to women for the first time in the 1970s. Pat Schroeder, Elizabeth Holtzman, Barbara Jordan, and Bella Abzug were elected to serve in Congress. The first two female United States Army generals were appointed in 1970, and the FBI hired its first female agents—Joanne Pierce and Susan Roley—in 1972. Also in 1972, Gloria Steinem published the first issue of *Ms.* magazine, a publication that dealt with feminist issues. Feminists believed that the term *Ms.* was preferable to *Miss* and *Mrs.* because women, just like men, should not have to be identified according to their marital status.

Fashion Allows Variety

The do-your-own-thing philosophy of the 1960s counterculture had a big influence on the fashion of the 1970s. An amazing variety of styles was available. Women could choose the supershort miniskirt of the 1960s, the longer hemline of the midiskirt, or long peasant skirts. These were sometimes worn with drawstring blouses, vests, and boots to create a western look.

Women also wore all kinds of pants, from velvet hot pants to tailored pants with a short jacket. Hot pants were tight fitting, extremely short shorts. A typical winter look was hot pants and long boots beneath an overcoat. Many companies did not allow their female employees to wear hot pants to work. By the late 1970s, a more conventional feminine look became popular again. Women wore long graceful skirts, printed shawls, sundresses, and elegant evening wear.

Bella Abzug served in the House of Representatives from 1973 to 1977.

Changes in Denim

Young men and women in the early 1970s continued to wear the ragged denim blue jeans, army fatigues, cotton T-shirts, and long hair popular in the late 1960s. Often their blue jeans were decorated with peace symbols. Many young women who were aiming for a natural look did not use makeup or lipstick. The word unisex was often used to describe this generation's antifashion approach to dress.

But some people wanted to stand out from the crowd. For them, designers such as Calvin Klein created special blue jeans decorated with rhinestones or silver studs. Some came with matching jackets. Sold in high-fashion boutiques, the so-called designer jeans were very expensive.

Leisure Wear and Funky Fashion

In the mid-1970s, menswear entered a peacock period. Brightly colored polyester leisure wear with purple, rose, orange, and green patterns became popular. Influenced by the dress styles of rock musicians, some men and women took to wearing platform shoes. The heels of these shoes could be as high as seven inches. Various kinds of leisure clothes also became popular. On the weekends, many men wore jogging suits—even those who had never jogged in their lives and had no intention of ever jogging.

Another new leisure fashion look emerged from the disco scene. Discotheques—disco dance clubs—had appeared in cities all over the country, and people flocked to them. Many people were influenced by the disco fashion styles seen in the 1977 movie *Saturday Night Fever*, which starred John Travolta. When going out to dance, men often wore a two- or three-piece outfit called a leisure suit. It consisted of a jacket, dress pants, and sometimes a vest. White was a favorite color. Plaid was also considered stylish. Women typically wore blouses with skirts or slacks. Most dress shirts had wide collars. Clothing was often made from an artificial fiber called polyester.

The disco era did not last long. It drew to a close as the decade ended.

The Popularity of CB Radios

Someone wishing to transmit a message over a CB (citizen band) radio would begin his or her broadcast with the words "breaker, breaker." In the mid-1970s, millions of Americans were uttering these words. People used their CB radios to contact other CB radio operators within a range of about four to five miles. CB radios first became available in 1947 but did not become popular until 1973. That was the year the federal government mandated a national speed limit of

55 miles per hour. Long-distance truckers tried to get around this new law by using CB radios to warn each other of the whereabouts of Smokies, their name for highway police officers. Once the media began reporting the truckers' use of CBs and the colorful jargon they used in their broadcasts, millions of people all around the country rushed out to buy CBs. Even First Lady Betty Ford owned a CB and transmitted broadcasts under the name First Mama. At the height of the CB craze in 1976, $1 billion worth of CBs were sold. But interest in CB radios faded away just as quickly as it had arisen. By the end of the decade, sales of CBs had plummeted.

Mood Rings

For Americans who were turning inward in 1975, what better way to explore their own feelings than to wear a mood ring? Millions of Americans, including Hollywood stars such as Sophia Loren and Paul Newman, did just that. The original mood stone ring was created and sold by Joshua Reynolds. Soon dozens of imitators began selling products with such names as impulse ring and persona ring. Mood rings were available in every price range from $2 to $250.

The mood stone was made of liquid crystals encased within clear quartz. The stone was able to change its color to supposedly show the mood of the person wearing the ring. For example, blue indicated happy feelings and reddish brown indicated feelings of insecurity. The liquid crystals were heat sensitive and actually responded to changes in body temperature rather than mood.

Pet Rocks

In 1975, more than a million Americans spent four dollars each to buy a most unusual pet—a pet rock! Gary Dahl placed smooth egg-shaped stones in boxes designed by a friend. Here was the perfect pet—one that did not make a mess, did not need special training, and did not need to be fed. Dahl said that Americans were tired of all the troubles in the world. They needed a good laugh, and that is precisely what the pet rock provided.

Entertainment and the Arts

With all the gloom and doom in the world, Americans in the 1970s just wanted an escape. They could forget their cares taking in a blockbuster at the local movie theater, listening to some easy music, or hitting the dance floor at the local disco.

Hollywood's Biggest Hits

DVR, streaming devices, and DVDs did not yet exist in the 1970s. Video players, known as VCRs, were new, and few families owned one. People flocked to theaters to see movies. Hollywood scored some of its biggest hits during this decade.

The Godfather debuted in 1972. Based on the novel by Mario Puzo, *The Godfather* told the story of an Italian-American crime family, the Corleones. It was a violent but excellent movie. *The Godfather* received the Academy Award for Best Picture. Today, some people still consider it one of the best films ever made. Two successful sequels would follow in 1974 and 1990.

Jaws was also based on a novel. Peter Benchley's book was about a giant killer shark. Hollywood released *Jaws* in 1975. Its eerie music

Marlon Brando gave an iconic performance in The Godfather.

and gripping images thrilled moviegoers. Some viewers found *Jaws* so scary that they avoided the beach that summer.

The original *Star Wars* movie came out in 1977. The science fiction film by George Lucas featured hero Luke Skywalker and villain Darth Vader. There were also aliens, lovable robots, and dazzling space battles. *Star Wars* earned more money than any previous film in Hollywood history. The movie also created a marketing frenzy. People snapped up books, action figures, costumes, and other merchandise related to the movie. This was not yet a popular practice.

Like *Star Wars* and *Jaws*, *Close Encounters of the Third Kind* (1977) was a big-budget film that used daring new special effects. Another popular hit was *Grease* (1978), which evoked nostalgia for the supposedly simpler time of the 1950s. *Superman: The Movie* (1978) and *Rocky* (1976), two other big movies of the 1970s, were stories about heroes. In very different ways, these films were about good guys fighting bad guys and winning. They focused on a search for a hero, which was something that seemed to be missing in American life.

Television of the 1970s

Many of the television shows of the 1970s reflected nostalgia for earlier decades. Such TV shows included *Happy Days* and *Laverne and Shirley*, which fondly remembered the 1950s. *Little House on the Prairie* celebrated the simple pleasures of frontier living, and *The Waltons* was set in Depression-era America.

One television show of the 1970s, however, dared to confront modern problems. Norman Lear's sitcom *All in the Family*, about the bigoted character Archie Bunker, dealt with issues such as racial prejudice, abortion, and feminism. *All in the Family* showed how families coped with such issues, but it usually did so in a comical way. America was so taken with this comedy that the show spawned several popular

"Live from New York, it's Saturday Night!"

That now-familiar phrase was first exclaimed on October 11, 1975, when *NBC's Saturday Night* debuted. The ninety-minute program began as a live variety show that featured musical numbers, short films, and comedy sketches performed by The Not Ready for Prime Time Players—John Belushi, Dan Aykroyd (on the left), Gilda Radner, Chevy Chase, Jane Curtin, Laraine Newman, and Garrett Morris.

The show, later renamed *Saturday Night Live*, was created to fill a hinterland time slot previously filled by reruns of Johnny Carson's *Tonight Show*. The cast often joked that no one was watching, but almost immediately it became essential weekend viewing. Some of *Saturday Night Live's* most successful alumni include Steve Martin (on the right), Bill Murray, Eddie Murphy, Julia Louis-Dreyfus, Adam Sandler, Will Ferrell, Amy Poehler, and Chris Rock. Now informally known as *SNL*, the show celebrated its fortieth anniversary in 2015 and shows no signs of stopping.

Gifted musician Jimi Hendrix died from a drug overdose in 1970.

sitcoms that also focused on social issues, including *The Jeffersons*, *Maude*, and *Good Times*.

Tragedies in the Music World

By the early to mid-1970s, it was apparent that the counterculture's greatest days had passed. The music scene in the 1970s was filled with tragic events and disappointing developments, such as the breakup of the Beatles. In 1970 and 1971, three of rock's top performers died from drug abuse.

Jimi Hendrix grew up in Seattle, Washington. A guitar prodigy, his music was fiery and dramatic. Hendrix is best remembered for his hit song "Purple Haze." At Woodstock in 1969, he performed a blistering version of the national anthem with his guitar. A year later, Jimi Hendrix died of a drug overdose. He was only twenty-seven years old.

Born in Texas in 1943, Janis Joplin ran away from home at seventeen to use her powerful voice. Joplin became a star after performing in the Monterey Pop Festival in 1967. She died three years later from a heroin overdose.

Jim Morrison was the lead singer of the Doors. The Florida native also wrote poetry. The Doors had an explosive sound. Their first album contained the number-one hit "Light My Fire." In 1971, Jim Morrison was in France when he died, probably from an overdose of heroin. Like Joplin and Hendrix, he was just twenty-seven years old.

The deaths seemed to keep coming. In 1974, Cass Elliott of the Mamas and the Papas died. Elvis Presley, The King of Rock 'n' Roll, died in 1977.

The effect of the deaths of these famous musicians was greater than the passing of any one individual. Part of the effect was a loss of the energy and excitement that had drawn together a whole generation during the decade before.

Music of the 1970s

As people of the 1970s focused on their own pursuits, some music seemed to reflect this phenomenon. People responded enthusiastically to the mellow, laid-back music of artists such as James Taylor, Barry Manilow, John Denver, Linda Ronstadt, Barbra Streisand, Anne Murray, and Carly Simon. These artists sang tunes about love and loss on a personal level instead of a broad political level as many of their 1960s predecessors had done.

Some higher energy groups and individual artists, however, continued to attract a devoted following. Among them were the Rolling Stones, the Who, the Grateful Dead, Bruce Springsteen, and Aerosmith. Groups such as Led Zeppelin, featuring loud and fast guitar work, were called heavy metal groups.

A kind of folk rock, played by such stars as Bob Dylan, Joni Mitchell, Paul Simon, and Billy Joel, focused on real life issues and hardships and was also popular during the 1970s.

Black soul music, which had attracted many fans during the 1960s, continued to be popular in the 1970s. Aretha Franklin, Al Green, Marvin Gaye, Stevie Wonder, Gladys Knight and the Pips, the Jackson Five, and Smokey Robinson and the Miracles, were among the biggest soul stars.

Other types of music also became popular during the 1970s. Jamaican musicians, such as Bob Marley and Jimmy Cliff, created a style of music known as reggae. Jazz musicians, such as Miles Davis, Chick Corea, and Herbie Hancock, created a jazz-rock type of music. It featured extensive use of newly available electronic instruments.

The Disco Craze

Perhaps the biggest new trend in music in the 1970s was disco, which appeared in the middle of the decade. Disco music featured a steady pulsing beat and catchy tunes. Lyrics focused on love, sex, and the

James Taylor's sweet voice and mellow guitar comforted listeners.

California Cuisine

Health-conscious Americans had a brand new cuisine to enjoy in the 1970s. Alice Waters (center foreground) opened her Chez Panisse restaurant in Berkeley, California, in 1971. She developed an imaginative new approach to cooking based on the use of the freshest and purest ingredients. Many of the foods were grown in her own garden and on local farms and ranches. Waters's restaurant became very popular with diners and remains so to this day. Her healthful and nutritious style of food preparation soon became known as California cuisine. Dishes were put together with creative combinations of ingredients that were chosen to enhance natural flavors, such as black and white sesame seed seared ahi tuna with hot and sour raspberry sauce. Meats, fish, and poultry were typically seared on a grill to lock in the flavors and keep the food moist and tender. Before long, California cuisine began appearing in other parts of the country, as well.

excitement of disco dancing. The disco style avoided the heavy topics of politics and hardship that had been popular in the 1960s. Disco was great for dancing and offered a temporary escape into fantasy and sensuality for millions of Americans who were ready for just that. The wild styles and carefree attitudes associated with disco appealed to young Americans who were tired of the years of political and social protest of the 1960s and early 1970s. Donna Summer, whose career took off after the success of her sexy hit "Love to Love You Baby," was one of the most popular disco artists.

Nightclubs filled with patrons eager to try the latest disco steps. A mirrored ball usually hung overhead. It splashed patterns of light across a colorful dance floor. The film *Saturday Night Fever*, released in 1977, came to symbolize the disco era. It starred John Travolta as a poor but talented dancer. Many scenes showed people doing disco dances like the Hustle. *Saturday Night Fever* featured songs by popular disco artists, including the Bee Gees and KC and the Sunshine Band. The film's soundtrack quickly became a top-selling album. In 1978, at the height of the disco craze, thirty-six million Americans danced the night away to the driving disco beat and flashing lights in twenty thousand discotheques, or disco clubs, all around the country.

Billie Jean King fought for women's equality on the court and off.

Sports

During this Me Generation, Americans focused on getting in shape. Jogging became a popular way to stay fit. In addition, tennis courts across the country were suddenly filled with people inspired by the new popularity of the classic sport.

Billie Jean King

In 1966, Billie Jean King won the singles tennis title in the women's division at the Wimbledon Championship Tournament in England. She was stunned when she was handed her prize—a gift certificate for clothes. In 1970, she was the women's division winner of the Open Tennis Tournament in Rome, where her $600 prize was considerably less than the $7,500 awarded to the winner of the men's division. Then in 1972 at the US Open, she won $10,000 while the men's champion, Ilie Nastase, won $25,000.

King was outraged by such unfairness, and she became determined to do something about it. In the summer of 1973, she accepted a tennis challenge from former Wimbledon champion Bobby Riggs in which the winner would receive $100,000. The match was promoted as a Battle of the Sexes. Riggs turned out to be no match for King, who easily defeated him in front of forty million television viewers. In 1973, King helped form a union known as the Women's Tennis Association (WTA), to fight for the rights of women tennis players. Thanks to her efforts, women's tennis began to be taken just as seriously as men's.

Arthur Ashe Helps Break the Color Barrier in Tennis

On July 5, 1975, tennis player Arthur Ashe became the first African American to win the Wimbledon men's singles tournament. Throughout his career, Ashe had faced racial discrimination. He had developed his talents playing in segregated parks in his hometown of Richmond, Virginia. When he beat tennis pro Jimmy Connors at Wimbledon in 1975, Ashe made progress toward breaking the color barrier in professional tennis.

Terrorists Strike the Olympics

Political turmoil and violence had plagued the Middle East for decades. The main conflict was the struggle between Israel and its Arab neighbors. The Jewish people of Israel and the Arabs who lived in surrounding nations were frequently at odds over the issue of who was the rightful owner of the Holy Land, a territory with great religious meaning for Jews, Muslims, and Christians. Acts of terrorism were frequent. But in the 1970s, this unrest affected more than politics.

The 1972 Summer Olympics in Munich, West Germany, began with much fanfare but ended in tragedy. On the morning of September 5, 1972, eight men from the Palestinian terrorist group Black September slipped into the Olympic Village in Munich and broke into apartments occupied by members of the Israeli wrestling and weight-lifting teams. Two of the Israelis tried to bar the door but were shot and killed. Nine others were taken hostage.

Arthur Ashe made strides for diversity in professional tennis.

Hammerin' Hank Aaron

During the 1970s, baseball player Hank Aaron chased the all-time home run record. Born in Alabama in 1934, Aaron got his start in the Negro leagues and broke into the major leagues in 1954. The outfielder quickly established himself as a consistent .300 hitter. Aaron played most of his major league years for the Milwaukee (eventually Atlanta) Braves.

By the end of the 1972-1973 season, Aaron approached but did not surpass Babe Ruth's career record of 714 home runs. The feat stirred much excitement in baseball but also brought Aaron death threats and racist hatred from fans who didn't want to see Ruth's record broken. On baseball's opening day in 1974, Aaron tied Ruth's record. Two games after that, on April 8, 1974, he blasted his 715th homer and became baseball's all-time home run king at the age of forty. He finished his career in 1976 with 755 homers. Aaron's record held until 2007, when it was broken by Barry Bonds.

Around the world, television viewers watched in horror. Overnight, the joy of the Olympics gave way to a deadly crisis. The terrorists demanded the release of hundreds of their comrades from Israeli prisons. Israel refused. As the day wore on, German police officers planned a rescue attempt. However, their plan was ruined when TV news cameras showed them sneaking into position. The terrorists saw the police on live television and warned them away.

The Black September terrorists demanded to be flown out of Germany. Two helicopters carried them and their hostages to a nearby airport to board a jet. At the airport, German police made another rescue attempt by positioning snipers to shoot the terrorists as they crossed the runway. The terrorists shot back. They also killed the nine remaining hostages. As the fighting at the airport raged, a German police officer and five of the terrorists were killed. The other three terrorists were captured.

In the wake of the bloodshed, Olympic officials debated canceling the rest of the Munich Games but decided that quitting would be a victory for terrorism. Instead, a memorial service was held to honor the eleven Israeli victims. The Olympics then somberly continued.

Most nations, and even some other radical groups, condemned Black September's attack on the Olympics. In the months that followed the Munich attack, Israeli agents hunted down and killed members of Black September. By 1974, the terrorist organization was no longer operating.

Muhammad Ali: The Greatest

"Float like a butterfly, sting like a bee" was one of the ways Muhammad Ali described his boxing technique. Born Cassius Clay, Ali referred to himself as the Greatest. As heavyweight champion in the 1960s, he had spoken out against the war in Vietnam. As a Black Muslim, Ali refused to be drafted into the army, and he was convicted

The Olympic flag flew at half-mast to commemorate the victims of the terrorist attack.

Mark Spitz

Terrorism spoiled the festive mood of the 1972 Olympics. Yet there were still some amazing athletic feats. An American swimmer named Mark Spitz set four world records. He also earned seven gold medals. No Olympic athlete had ever won so many gold medals at once.

The twenty-two-year-old Spitz came from California. He had been competing as a swimmer since the age of eight. As a teen, Spitz set several world records. He specialized in the freestyle and butterfly events.

At the Munich Olympics, Spitz was in peak form. He won four solo events. He also led the US swim team to victory in three relay events.

of draft evasion. His license to box and his title were taken away from him. But in 1970, the United States Supreme Court overturned the ruling. Before long, Ali was back in the ring. After several tough bouts, he regained his title in a fight called the Rumble in the Jungle against George Foreman in 1974.

A Motorcycle Daredevil

Perhaps the most unusual sports figure of the 1970s was Evel Knievel. Known as America's Legendary Daredevil, Knievel became famous for his amazing death-defying stunts. Among his best-known stunts were his motorcycle jumps over multiple cars and buses, which he continued despite several serious crashes and injuries. In October 1975, Knievel successfully jumped his motorcycle over fourteen Greyhound buses in Ohio. Like many of his other feats, this performance was televised and some 52 percent of Americans were watching as Knievel performed.

Muhammad Ali came back into the boxing ring in 1970.

National and International Politics

President Lyndon Johnson announced that he would not run for reelection in 1968. He knew that the voters would not reelect him. They blamed him for the long war in Vietnam, which was being fought to keep the communist North Vietnamese from taking over South Vietnam.

Vietnamization

Richard Nixon was the Republican presidential candidate. He told the American people what they wanted to hear. Nixon promised to end the war with honor and to bring Americans together—to heal the divisions in American society caused by the war. Nixon narrowly defeated Hubert Humphrey in the 1968 election. By the time he was inaugurated, many American people were voicing opposition to the war. He knew that the longer the war dragged on, the more difficult it would be to accomplish anything else. His military advisors said that it could take many more years to win the war, and it would require larger numbers of American troops. The American people would not stand for this.

Nixon's plan was to pass responsibility to the South Vietnamese.

Americans' opposition to the war became stronger with every atrocity.

Nixon and his advisors briefly considered using nuclear weapons to end the war quickly. This, however, appeared too risky. Nixon also knew, as Johnson had, that to withdraw suddenly from the war in an obvious defeat would be political suicide. So Nixon decided on a plan of Vietnamization.

Under Vietnamization, more responsibility for fighting the war would be turned over to the South Vietnamese forces. Gradually, American troops would be withdrawn. Then, with the United States cheering on the troops from the sidelines, the South Vietnamese would be free to defeat the North Vietnamese on their own.

The Vietnamization strategy never really had much chance of success. The South Vietnamese government was too corrupt, and the South Vietnamese Army was too weak to fight well without the help of better trained and equipped American soldiers. In April 1970, Nixon ordered American troops into eastern Cambodia to attack North Vietnamese forces. Most of the North Vietnamese withdrew without a fight. This invasion succeeded only in making an already unstable political situation in Cambodia even worse. It would lead to the communist takeover of that country by the fanatical Pol Pot and his Khmer Rouge. Pol Pot would go on to murder up to one million of his countrymen in the killing fields of Cambodia. Nixon's invasion of Cambodia would also lead to tragic events much closer to home.

War Protest Turns Deadly

On April 30, 1970, the day Nixon announced the American invasion of Cambodia, antiwar protests erupted at college campuses across the nation. Outraged students cried out for peace.

Like most colleges, Kent State was a hub of antiwar feelings. On May 1, 1970, there was a riot in the city of Kent. The city's mayor requested that the Ohio National Guard be sent to his city to prevent further disturbances. On May 2, about a thousand Ohio National

Antiwar Sentiment Peaks

As the war dragged on into the early 1970s, the number of people who thought US troops should leave Vietnam grew. Two news stories in the early 1970s fanned public outrage over the war.

First, Americans learned of an incident that had occurred earlier in Vietnam. In March 1968, US soldiers had attacked the village of My Lai. They killed up to five hundred unarmed civilians there. An army officer named William Calley led the soldiers. In 1971, he was tried and convicted for the killings at My Lai. People were shocked by the grisly details of the My Lai massacre. They were also angry that army officers had tried to keep the massacre a secret.

Another secret about the war was revealed in 1971. Newspaper reporters, such as Ben Bradlee *(pictured)*, learned of the Pentagon Papers. The Pentagon Papers were top-secret government files. They showed that the US government had sometimes lied about the Vietnam War. For example, top government officials had insisted for years that America was winning the war. But as the Pentagon Papers revealed, many officials did not believe the war could be won.

President Nixon tried to keep newspapers from printing the Pentagon Papers. However, the US Supreme Court ruled that they could. The release of the Pentagon Papers fueled further antiwar sentiment. By 1973, seven out of ten Americans opposed the war.

Guardsmen arrived in Kent. Most took up positions on Kent State University's campus. Around noon on May 4, a large crowd of students assembled for a peaceful protest on campus. When approximately one hundred National Guardsmen ordered the protestors to leave, some of the students hurled rocks. Finally, some of the Guardsmen fired their rifles into the crowd. Four students were killed. Nine more were wounded.

Just ten days later, a similar incident took place in Mississippi. Police shot and killed two students at Jackson State College. Americans were horrified by these events, and opposition to the war became stronger than ever.

The National Voting Age Is Lowered

The post-World War II baby boom had created a huge population of young people in the 1960s and 1970s. Throughout the Vietnam War, these young people had made their voices heard by protesting the war and advocating new ideals for society. But until 1971, these young political activists could not vote unless they were over the age of twenty-one. Partly because of the outspoken attitude of American youths during this period and partly in an effort to give young people the opportunity to fight for changes through the ballot box rather than violence, the Twenty-Sixth Amendment to the Constitution was ratified in the summer of 1971, which lowered the national voting age to eighteen. From then on, even teens would have a chance to help elect their government representatives.

US Troops Leave Vietnam

In February 1970, National Security Advisor Henry Kissinger had begun secret negotiations aimed at ending the Vietnam War with the

North Vietnamese. By 1972, the talks—no longer secret—were continuing, as was the war. But it seemed as though progress was being made. The number of American troops in Vietnam was steadily decreasing. Hoping to win another term in office in the 1972 election, Nixon wanted to be seen as a peacemaker. In February of that year, Nixon became the first American president to visit China. In May, he became the first United States president to visit the Soviet Union. While he was there, he signed nuclear weapons treaties. Nixon seemed to be doing all the right things. In November, American voters handed Nixon a landslide reelection victory over George McGovern.

In December, the peace talks with the North Vietnamese broke down. Nixon ordered a massive bombing of North Vietnam. By January 1973, the peace talks were on again, and on January 27, an agreement was signed. By March 29, 1973, the last American troops had left South Vietnam. The war continued without the help of American soldiers. By April 1975, when Saigon, the South Vietnamese capital, fell to North Vietnam, all American advisors and other personnel had left South Vietnam. The Vietnam War quickly ended when North Vietnam took over South Vietnam.

President Nixon Resigns

On June 17, 1972, five men were arrested for breaking into the Democratic National Committee headquarters at the Watergate hotel-office complex in Washington, D.C. Two reporters for the *Washington Post*, Carl Bernstein and Bob Woodward, began covering the story. They traced connections between the burglars and President Nixon's reelection committee largely through an anonymous source known only as Deep Throat. They published reports about their progress. Eventually, their work would lead to televised hearings of the Senate Watergate Committee in 1973. All of Nixon's top advisors had to

Richard Nixon resigned in the wake of the Watergate scandal.

Nixon Goes to China

In 1949, China became a communist country. It was called the People's Republic of China. Shortly after, US and Chinese soldiers clashed in the Korean War. In the two decades that followed, America and China remained wary of each other. The United States did not even recognize the People's Republic as the legitimate government of China. Then, in 1972, the two countries took steps toward friendship. President Nixon made a historic trip to China. He met with Chinese leader Mao Zedong and Chinese Premier Chou-En-Lai (pictured). They agreed to peaceful relations between their nations.

President Nixon's trip made world headlines. No US president had ever before gone to the People's Republic of China. Although not a superpower, China was the most populous nation in the world. Nixon's visit worried the Soviet Union. A friendship with China, which borders the Soviet Union, would give America an advantage in the Cold War. This concern spurred Soviet interest in détente with the United States.

testify. Each had played a role in the scandal, and evidence pointed to Nixon's involvement in authorizing a cover-up of the illegal break-in. High administration officials, including Attorney General John Mitchell, Special Counsel John Dean, Chief of Staff H.R. Haldeman, and Domestic Advisor John Ehrlichman, were sentenced to prison terms.

The Watergate affair revealed a shocking degree of corruption in the Nixon administration. In a separate scandal, Vice President Spiro Agnew was forced to resign in 1973. He was accused of accepting bribes and kickbacks while serving as governor of Maryland, and he was charged with federal income tax evasion. Gerald Ford was appointed vice president to replace Agnew.

In May 1973, Archibald Cox was appointed special prosecutor to investigate the Watergate affair. As other presidents had done in the past, Nixon had secretly taped conversations that took place in the White House. When Cox ordered Nixon to turn over the tapes, Nixon had Cox fired. Acting Attorney General Robert Bork then appointed Leon Jaworski as Cox's replacement.

In July 1974, the Supreme Court ordered Nixon to turn over the tapes to the special prosecutor. The tapes proved that Nixon had lied about the cover-up. He now faced impeachment. On August 8, he announced his decision to resign the presidency. The next day, Vice President Gerald Ford became president. It was the first time in US history that a person became the nation's chief executive without being elected president or vice president. On September 8, Ford granted Nixon a pardon for any crimes he might have committed while in office. Ford's popularity in opinion polls immediately dropped from 71 percent to 49 percent.

Women's Rights

There were, of course, issues that mattered to people besides Watergate. One of the most important was the women's rights movement. Women wanted to have the same kinds of job opportunities as men, and they wanted equal pay for equal work. At the beginning of the decade, women earned about 57 percent of what men earned for the same work. Feminists believed a new law that would protect women's rights and end discrimination had become necessary.

The struggle for congressional passage and ratification of the Equal Rights Amendment (ERA) was led by the National Organization for Women (NOW). The ERA stated, "Equality of rights under the law shall not be denied or abridged by the United States or by any state on account of sex." Congress passed the ERA in 1972, but in order to become part of the Constitution it also had to be ratified, or approved, by three fourths of the states. Ultimately, the ERA went down in defeat. A major milestone in women's rights involved the issue of abortion. In 1973, the United States Supreme Court ruled in *Roe v. Wade* that laws prohibiting abortion violated a woman's right of privacy. This proved to be a very controversial ruling, and this issue is still up for debate today.

The 1976 Presidential Election

The presidential election in 1976 was a close race between Gerald Ford and Jimmy Carter, a peanut farmer from Georgia. Both men appealed to voters as nice, decent, honest men—a welcome contrast to Nixon and his administration. Carter won the election.

Carter tried to get Americans to face a harsh new economic reality. He said that because there were limits to available energy resources in the world, energy costs would become increasingly more expensive. Carter asked Americans to save energy wherever possible. To set a good example, Carter announced that he was keeping the White

THIRD WORLD WOMENS
HE MOST EXPLOITED &
OPPRESSED IN THE HU-
MAN RACE.

THIRD WORLD
WOMEN'S ALLIANCE

Women fought for equal rights and celebrated the passage of the ERA.

Democrat Jimmy Carter was elected president in 1976.

House thermostat at 68°F. Carter would often appear on television in the White House wearing a thick sweater to show that he was saving energy by using less heat. Carter's message did not go over well with Americans.

Returning the Panama Canal

President Carter was unpopular with many Americans because of the poor economic conditions that reigned during his administration. He did, however, have some significant achievements during his term as president. Among them was the Panama Canal Treaty of 1977.

Since 1914, when the canal was completed by American construction crews, the United States had run the Panama Canal. Over time, the local people of Panama came to resent the United States presence. They began to protest and demanded that the Panama Canal Zone, where the canal is located, be returned to Panama. As unrest grew worse in the 1970s, President Carter decided to take action. In 1977, Carter and Panamanian Head of State Omar Torrijos Herrera signed a treaty. It provided for the return of the canal to Panama on December 31, 1999. The agreement met with mixed reactions. Some Americans were angry to lose such an important possession. Others, however, considered it a diplomatic triumph for Carter.

A Stagnant Economy

To make matters worse, there was a new problem in the American economy. Inflation, or rising prices for items, combined with high unemployment and a stagnant economy to create what was called stagflation. Partly due to the higher cost of oil and other resources, the economy was no longer growing as rapidly as it had been in earlier years. In addition, the size of the workforce had increased tremendously, to some degree because more women were looking for jobs outside the home. With so many people needing jobs, the economy could not grow fast enough to make room for everyone. As a result, there was widespread unemployment.

The Cold War Thaws

The Cold War was a fierce rivalry between the United States and the Soviet Union that had begun after World War II. Neither side trusted the other. Both nations constantly feared a sneak attack. In 1962, the United States and the Soviet Union had come dangerously close to a nuclear war after the Soviets placed missiles in Cuba. By the 1970s, both sides were eager to reduce the tension.

US and Soviet leaders began holding talks. They discussed key issues, such as nuclear weapons and human rights. Both nations agreed to limit the number of nuclear missiles they kept. They also agreed to trade more goods with each other. The Soviet Union bought large amounts of US wheat. This new spirit of cooperation was called détente. It is a French word meaning to relax or to ease.

The US and Soviet space programs also joined forces. They launched a joint mission in space. In 1975, orbiting US and Soviet spacecraft docked together. Astronauts from both countries shook hands while floating high above earth. The Apollo-Soyuz mission offered hope for better relations between the two superpowers.

But the era of détente did not last long. By the end of the 1970s, America and the Soviet Union were once again enemies. The fear and hatred of the Cold War returned.

Soviet Troops Invade Afghanistan

In 1979, the Soviet Union invaded Afghanistan. A nine-year war followed. The Soviet invasion of Afghanistan had a major impact

The Apollo-Soyuz was the first joint US–Soviet space flight.

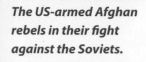

The US-armed Afghan rebels in their fight against the Soviets.

on world events. For decades, the Soviet Union had meddled in Afghan affairs. In 1978, a pro-Soviet communist party seized power in Afghanistan, but the Afghans rose up to oust that government. By 1979, Afghanistan's communist government was in trouble and called for help from the Soviet Union. Soviet leaders responded by ordering a large invasion and seizing the capital of Kabul and other cities. Afghan fighters were unable to stop the Soviets. The poorly armed fighters fled to the mountains.

The United States protested the Soviet invasion of Afghanistan. America and the Soviet Union were still Cold War rivals. US officials feared that the Soviets might be planning more invasions in Asia. President Carter took steps to show his ire. He canceled all sales of US wheat to the Soviet Union and boycotted the 1980 Moscow Olympics.

The US government took another step. It secretly began helping the Afghan rebels hiding in the mountains by shipping them weapons and supplies so they could fight the Soviets. The rebels were devoted believers in Islam and viewed their struggle against the Soviets as a holy war. The rebels called themselves *mujahideen*, or holy warriors. After years of bitter fighting, they would defeat the Soviet army—with consequences that are still felt today.

The Nation Endures an Oil Crisis

Because America was so dependent on foreign oil, Americans faced a serious fuel problem when gasoline prices skyrocketed during the 1970s. To punish Western nations, such as the United States, for supporting Israel in its war against its Arab neighbors, the Arab nations of the Oil Producing and Exporting Countries (OPEC) started an oil embargo. They forced Americans to pay very high prices in order to buy the oil needed to run cars and other machinery. The lack of oil caused many problems in the United States. It became very costly to heat a home or run a business. Some factories laid off workers. There was also a shortage of gas. Drivers were allowed to fill up their cars only on certain days. Lines at gas stations were sometimes blocks long.

For many years, Americans had enjoyed driving their big cars, known as gas guzzlers. When the price of gasoline shot up to the seemingly astronomical price of more than a dollar a gallon, many Americans looked for ways to make driving more economical. The compact cars of Japanese and German auto manufacturers became popular with American consumers. The big three American auto-makers—Ford, General Motors, and Chrysler—scrambled to produce their own version of the compact car. More than a quarter of a million Americans bought the new motorized bicycle known as a moped. The Department of Transportation had approved the use of mopeds in 1973. The moped was a truly economical means of transportation, as it was capable of getting one hudnred fifty miles to a gallon of gas.

In March 1974, the Arab nations started shipping oil again. The crisis passed. However, America's need for foreign oil would cause many more problems in the future. To help ease its reliance on for-eign oil, the United States authorized the development of oil fields on Alaska's Arctic coast. The huge Prudhoe Bay oil field is the largest in North America. Oil began flowing through the 800-mile Trans-Alaska Pipeline once the three-year project was completed in 1977.

Progress in the Middle East

The Middle East had been a hotbed of problems for decades, as Arabs fought Israel over what both groups considered holy land. On October 6, 1973, Egypt and Syria carried out a surprise attack on Israel on the holiest day of the Jewish calendar—Yom Kippur, the Day of Atonement. Israel won the war, but it suffered heavy losses because it had not been sufficiently prepared.

Gas became a precious commodity when OPEC raised prices.

Sadat, Carter, and Begin prepare to sign the Camp David Accords.

In 1977, Egyptian President Anwar Sadat decided that the time had come to make peace with Israel. He made a historic visit to Jerusalem to meet with Israeli Prime Minister Menachem Begin. Jimmy Carter then invited both leaders to come to Camp David, the presidential retreat in Maryland, where he offered to help them reach a peace agreement. Carter helped Sadat and Begin overcome numerous obstacles in their negotiations. The final peace agreement was signed in March 1979. Known as the Camp David Accords, this peace agreement was Jimmy Carter's greatest foreign policy triumph.

For their efforts, Sadat and Begin received the 1978 Nobel Peace Prize. However, some Arab nations broke off relations with Egypt because of the peace agreement with Israel. They kicked Egypt out of the Arab League, an organization of Arab states. In 1981, Egyptian terrorists shot and killed Anwar Sadat.

Terror in the Skies

In the late 1960s, terrorists began hijacking airplanes. Using weapons they had smuggled aboard, a small group of hijackers could take control of a plane, order the pilot to land, and state their demands in exchange for freeing their hostages. Many hijackings were carried out by members of Palestinian terrorist groups. The most famous of these groups was the Palestine Liberation Organization (PLO), which was headed by Yasser Arafat.

By the early 1970s, airline hijackings were a major problem around the world. Government officials had few choices once a plane had been hijacked. They could order soldiers or special police units to storm the aircraft, but that put hostages at great risk. Government officials could also choose to meet some of the terrorists' demands in exchange for the release of the hostages, but this might encourage future hijackings.

By the mid-1970s, governments had increased airport security to try to prevent hijackings. They installed X-ray machines in airports. These machines could reveal weapons hidden inside luggage.

Unlike some other countries, Israel always refused to meet hijackers' demands. On June 27, 1976, Palestinian terrorists hijacked a French airliner that had many Israelis aboard. They took the plane to Entebbe in Uganda. Uganda's dictator, Idi Amin, supported the terrorists. The terrorists threatened to kill the passengers if more than fifty Palestinian terrorists being held prisoner in five countries were not released. On July 3, 1976, a special unit of Israeli soldiers took off from Israel and flew more than two thousand miles to Entebbe. They fought off Ugandan soldiers, killed all the hijackers, and rescued more than one hundred passengers. Three hostages and the leader of the Israeli soldiers also died in the daring raid.

The Ayatollah Khomeini Americans Held Hostage in Iran

In November 1979, a crisis erupted in a different part of the Middle East—Iran. An Islamic revolution had swept the country early in 1979. Before the Iranian revolution, Shah Mohammad Reza Pahlavi ruled the country. The shah was very unpopular with his people because he ruled using threats and torture. Iranians also disliked his close ties with America. Over time, many Iranians came to believe that Iran's religious leaders should be in charge of the country. The Ayatollah Ruhollah Khomeini, an Islamic scholar, led the move toward revolution. As protesters filled the streets, the shah fled. Khomeini took control of Iran.

Although the shah no longer held power, Iranians still became outraged when the United States agreed to take in the ex-leader for cancer treatment. In November, a group of outraged Iranian students who supported the Ayatollah stormed the US embassy in Iran and

Yasser Arafat led the Palestine Liberation Organization.

Followers of the Ayatollah guard the besieged US embassy.

took sixty-six Americans hostage. The US government demanded the release of its citizens. Iran stubbornly refused, although they did release a few for medical and other reasons.

Throughout the next year, television viewers around the world watched the American captives being paraded before jeering crowds. The Iranians burned American flags and chanted anti-American slogans. By November 1980, fifty-two hostages were still being held. This situation proved to be a disaster for the Carter administration, which seemed unable to end the crisis. This was one major cause of Carter's defeat in the 1980 presidential election.

Advances in Science, Technology, and Medicine

Space exploration continued and thrived in the 1970s. At the same time, Americans became more concerned for the health of the earth as a new environmental movement sprang up.

The Space Program

Important milestones in the exploration of the solar system were achieved during the 1970s. Following the historic landing on the moon in 1969 by the astronauts of *Apollo 11*, NASA launched several more successful moon landings that ended with *Apollo 17* in 1972. In 1975, the United States and the Soviet Union, in a rare show of superpower cooperation, linked together an Apollo spacecraft with a Soviet Soyuz spacecraft for forty-four hours to form a temporary orbiting space station. Television viewers on earth were able to watch as American astronauts and Russian cosmonauts visited each other.

Unmanned spacecrafts were launched to many different parts of the solar system. The *Mariner*, *Voyager*, *Viking*, and *Pioneer* space probes sent information back to Earth from Mercury, Venus, Mars, Jupiter, and Saturn. In 1976, *Viking 1* and *Viking 2* orbited Mars. When the Viking landing crafts reached the surface of Mars, they began

The United States launched the Skylab space station in 1973.

The typical 1970s office computers were still quite large.

sending back amazingly clear full-color pictures of the rocky, desert-like Martian landscape. It was like a science-fiction story come true. The Viking landers also tested samples of Martian soil. Unfortunately, unlike science fiction, the Viking mission found no signs of Martian life.

In May 1973, another important event took place for the American space program. *Skylab*, the United States' first space station, was launched. *Skylab* was designed to orbit, or move around, earth at a distance of three hundred miles. Aboard the space station were astronauts who conducted scientific and medical experiments. *Skylab* was manned by three research crews before the astronauts left the space station and returned to earth in February 1974. Skylab was supposed to be able to continue to send information back to earth to help NASA continue its space research for many years to come. In 1979, however, *Skylab*'s orbit began to deteriorate. In July of that year, parts of the space station crashed in parts of Australia and in the Indian Ocean. Fortunately, no one was hurt. But the possibility of using *Skylab* to continue space exploration was over.

Personal Computers

Until the 1970s, computers were so expensive that only the largest corporations and government agencies could afford them. They were also so big that they occupied entire rooms. The first computers designed for use by individuals made their appearance in the mid-1970s. In 1975, a company called MITS created the Altair 8800. It cost only about four hundred dollars, but it came as a kit—the buyer had to assemble the machine.

Soon, other companies began selling fully assembled personal computers. In 1976, Steve Jobs and Steve Wozniak, two college dropouts, went to work in a garage and produced the Apple I, a crude version of a personal computer, or PC. In 1977, they began selling a better

Danger to the Ozone Layer

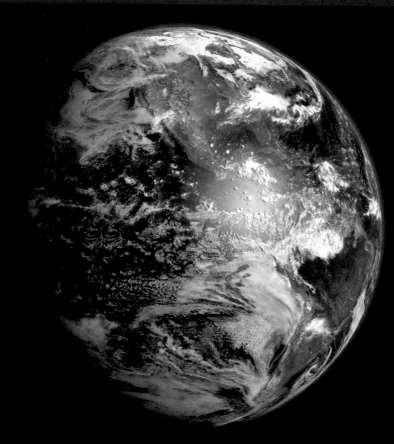

Science also gave the world some not-so-good news in the 1970s. In 1974, scientists announced that gases, known as chlorofluoro-carbons, or CFCs, which are given off by aerosol spray cans and other everyday items, were harmful to the ozone layer. The ozone layer of the atmosphere protects the earth from deadly ultraviolet radiation from the sun. The study predicted that further damage to the ozone layer could cause changes in the earth's weather, as well as increases in the number of skin cancer cases.

version, the Apple II. People snapped up the Apples as quickly as they could be built. By the end of the decade, Apple II computers could be found in millions of homes, offices, and schools.

At the same time, Bill Gates, another college dropout, founded Microsoft with his partner, Paul Allen. Bill Gates had developed an operating system for IBM to be used on the IBM PC. His new company, Microsoft, developed and sold PC operating system software and would eventually become America's biggest corporation—and Bill Gates would become America's richest man.

Apple, the company Steve Jobs (pictured) cofounded with Steve Wozniak, has continued to be at the forefront of consumer electronics innovation.

The First Test-Tube Baby

The 1970s also saw great breakthroughs in medicine. Until 1978, a woman with blocked fallopian tubes could not become pregnant. But in that year, Louise Brown, the world's first test-tube baby, was born in Oldham, England. An egg was taken from Louise's mother and placed in a petri dish. There, the egg was fertilized with Louise's father's sperm. When the fertilized egg had developed into an eight-celled embryo, it was implanted in the mother's uterus. A normal development of the fetus followed. Eventually, healthy five-pound, twelve-ounce Louise was born.

Louise Brown was the first child to be conceived using in vitro fertilization.

Tech Firsts

Aside from personal computers, the 1970s saw early versions of other electronic items that are well known today. The multibillion-dollar video game industry began humbly in 1972. That year, a company named Atari released the first commercially successful video game . Called Pong, it bore a vague resemblance to tennis. By today's standards, Pong's graphics would be laughable. Players hit a square ball with rectangular rackets that could move only up and down on the two-dimensional screen.

Today, many people like to listen to music on their phones or MP3 players as they work out, walk, or ride buses and trains. The first personal stereo system a person could carry around came out in 1979. Made by Sony, it was called the Walkman. It played cassette tapes.

Nuclear power became a concern after the Three Mile Island disaster.

Tragedy Avoided at Three Mile Island

Throughout the 1970s, disaster films about natural or man-made catastrophes were popular in America. Movies such as *The Poseidon Adventure*, *The Towering Inferno*, and *Earthquake* provided hours of escape from real-world disasters, such as the war in Vietnam.

Most people considered the events portrayed in disaster movies far-fetched, especially those in *The China Syndrome*, a 1979 film about an accident at a nuclear power plant. But on March 28, 1979, shortly after that film's release, the country had a real-life disaster that was as scary as anything on the big screen. Engineers at the Three Mile Island nuclear power plant in Pennsylvania noticed a mechanical problem with the cooling system, so they shut off the water to the reactor. Without water to keep it cool, the reactor quickly heated up and began to melt. Radiation began to leak outside. For a while, it looked as if a total meltdown might occur. Luckily, engineers were able to cool down the reactor. Still, there was great concern for the health of local residents despite government claims that the radiation released did not pose a threat.

President Jimmy Carter tried to calm people down by personally visiting the accident site to show that there was no longer any danger. Investigators found that the small amount of radiation that escaped was not enough to cause harm. Part of the plant was destroyed by the accident. The rest of it reopened after repairs and is still operating today.

Major antinuclear demonstrations were held after the Three Mile Island disaster. The result was a limit on the use and further construction of nuclear power plants, as well as a fear of nuclear accidents that continues even today.

To calm Americans' fears, President Carter and the First Lady personally visited the Three Mile Island facility.

Toxic Waste

Nuclear power plants were not the only source of potential environmental disasters. In the mid-1970s, residents in the Love Canal area of Niagara Falls, New York, began to notice chemical smells and strangely colored water seeping out of the ground. Chemicals began bubbling up in lawns and basements. The residents of Love Canal had a much higher rate of cancer and other diseases than did people in other neighborhoods. The Love Canal neighborhood was built on an area that had been used by Hooker Chemical Company to dump toxic

Toxic waste in the environment threatened the health of Americans.

The first Earth Day celebration took place in 1970.

chemical wastes in the 1930s and 1940s. Among these wastes was dioxin, one of the most toxic substances ever created. In July 1978, President Jimmy Carter declared Love Canal a federal disaster area. Fifteen million dollars was set aside for the relocation of Love Canal families. Sadly, there were about fifty thousand other toxic waste disposal sites all across America. There was now a new law mandating safe disposal of toxic wastes, but this came too late to help families living near these sites.

Celebrating and Protecting the Earth

The idea of returning to nature became popular in the 1970s. Aside from influencing art and lifestyles, it had an effect on government policy. In 1970, the Environmental Protection Agency (EPA) was created. It was set up to establish standards to prevent pollution from automobiles and industry and to protect Americans from the dangers of toxic chemicals and radioactive waste. It made the new outlook of taking care of nature an official part of the government.

This new awareness of the environment and the dangers that could be caused by pollution and waste helped create a new holiday. In April 1970, the first Earth Day celebration was held. It began as an effort to make all people take notice of the harm human beings have done to the environment throughout their history and to look at ways pollution and other problems can be corrected or prevented.

Conclusion

The 1970s were marked by several serious crises. These problems in the United States and around the world made the 1970s a time of upheaval and dissatisfaction with the way society and government worked.

The decade 1970 to 1979 was a tough time for the United States. Even as it was celebrating two hundred years since winning independence from Britain, the nation endured defeat in Vietnam—a war many didn't understand. Watergate caused many people to doubt their government. The crisis in the Middle East hit Americans at the gas station and made them fear airline travel. From Three Mile Island to Jonestown, there seemed to be nothing but bad news.

By the end of the decade, the American economy was struggling. Companies were closing and people were losing their jobs. The many problems created an uneasy sense of doubt. Some people wondered whether America's power was waning. People seemed to be disgusted with politics and government and sought to escape traditional ways of life.

Because of this desire for change, the 1970s were also marked by unusual fads and fashions, from the pet rock to disco. Many TV shows and movies harkened back to earlier eras, instilling nostalgia in the country for more innocent times. On the other end of the spectrum, many Americans tried to escape the realism of a sinking economy and hard times by wearing outlandish costumes and hitting the disco dance floor. Still others desperately turned to the comfort of drugs.

In November 1980, Ronald Reagan was elected president of the United States. His administration put bold new political and economic policies into place. These helped America to bounce back from its troubles of the 1970s. The economy improved, which created new jobs. The space shuttle made its first flight. Personal computers became available. America proved it was still a world leader in technology.

Yet the United States also experienced troubles during the 1980s. A deadly disease called AIDS killed millions of people. A new drug known as crack became the source of much suffering and violence in American cities. The gap between wealthy and poor Americans grew wider during the 1980s. In 1987, the US stock market crashed. Meanwhile, wars raged around the globe.

As the decade ended, the Cold War began to thaw. Soviet leader Mikhail Gorbachev tried to overhaul the Soviet government and economy. He also wanted to improve relations with the United States. But Gorbachev's reforms led to many changes. Soon, the Soviet Union would break apart, and the United States would be the world's only superpower.

The seeds for all of this activity were sown in the 1970s. From the political awareness inspired by opposition to the Vietnam War to the bell-bottoms and designer jeans of the fashion world, the 1970s were a decade that has continually shown its influence and will probably do so for many years to come.

Love them or hate them, the styles of the '70s are distinct and memorable.

Timeline

1970   Musicians Jimi Hendrix and Janis Joplin die. President Nixon orders the bombing of Cambodia. The Kent State shootings occur. The EPA is created. The first Earth Day is celebrated.

1971   Jim Morrison, lead singer of the Doors, dies. The Twenty-Sixth Amendment, which gives eighteen-year-olds the right to vote, is ratified.

1972   AIM seizes the Bureau of Indian Affairs. Gloria Steinem publishes first issue of *Ms.* Congress passes the ERA, but it fails to be ratified. The Watergate break-in occurs. Richard Nixon wins reelection to the presidency. The massacre of Israeli athletes at the Olympic Games is committed by Arab terrorists.

1973   AIM holds a protest against unfair treatment of Indians at Wounded Knee. Billie Jean King wins the US Open and defeats Bobby Riggs in the Battle of the Sexes. The *Roe v. Wade* decision protects the right to abortion. CB radios become popular. Billie Jean King helps form the Women's Tennis Association. United States troops pull out of Vietnam. The Senate Water-

gate Committee hearings are televised. Vice President Spiro Agnew resigns. Egypt and Syria attack Israel in Yom Kippur War. *Skylab* is launched.

1974 Indian Self-Determination Act is passed. Cass Elliott of the Mamas and the Papas dies. Muhammad Ali defeats George Foreman in the Rumble in the Jungle. President Richard Nixon resigns. Gerald Ford becomes president. CFCs are found to be harmful to the ozone layer.

1975 Mood rings go on sale. The pet rock becomes available. Muhammad Ali defeats Joe Frazier in the Thrilla in Manila. The United States and Soviet Union link an Apollo spacecraft with a Soyuz spacecraft. Arthur Ashe becomes the first African American to win the Wimbledon tennis tournament. Evel Knievel leaps fourteen Greyhound buses on his motorcycle.

1976 America celebrates its bicentennial anniversary. Writer Tom Wolfe describes the 1970s as the "Me Decade." Israeli soldiers rescue the passengers of a hijacked jetliner in Entebbe, Uganda. *Rocky* opens in theaters. Jimmy Carter is elected president. *Viking 1* and *Viking 2* orbit Mars. Steve Jobs and Steve Wozniak develop the Apple I.

1977 *Roots* miniseries premieres. *Saturday Night Fever* comes out in theaters. *Star Wars* premieres. Elvis Presley dies. President Carter signs the Panama Canal Treaty. Steve Wozniak and Steve Jobs begin selling the Apple II.

1978 In Jonestown, People's Temple cult members, led by Reverend Jim Jones, commit mass suicide. *Grease* opens in theaters. *Superman: The Movie* premieres. The disco craze reaches its height. The first test-tube baby is born. Camp David Accords are signed by Egypt and Israel.

1979 Cesar Chavez leads the strike for United Farm Workers Union. The Three Mile Island disaster occurs. Ayatollah Khomeini comes to power in Iran after overthrowing the Shah. Americans are taken hostage in Iran.

Glossary

bicentennial—Relating to a two-hundredth anniversary.

communist—A follower of a political and economic system in which all citizens are supposed to share work and property equally.

counterculture—A group or a culture that does not conform to the prevailing societal attitudes.

cult—A religious group with unusual beliefs and a controlling leader.

détente—A policy that promotes the relaxing of hostilities between nations.

embargo—A ban on trade.

embryo—Fertilized egg.

guru—Spiritual teacher or leader.

hijack—To seize control of a vehicle by force.

impeach—To bring formal charges of misconduct against an elected leader; if found guilty of those charges, the leader is removed from office.

kickback—Illicit payment made in exchange for a providing a particular service.

nuclear—Relating to energy that comes from the splitting or merging of atoms.

overdose—Too much of a drug taken at once.

radiation—Invisible but harmful rays and particles given off by nuclear materials.

radioactive—Emitting radiation.

superpower—A powerful country that leads other countries.

toxic—Poisonous.

Further Reading

Books

Lusted, Marcia Amidon. *The Three Mile Island Nuclear Disaster.* Minneapolis, Minn.: Abdo Publishing Company, 2012.

New York Times, *The Times of the Seventies.* New York, N.Y.: Black Dog & Leventhal Publishers, 2013.

Niven, Felicia Lowenstein. *Fabulous Fashions of the 1970s.* Berkeley Heights, N.J.: Enslow Publishers, 2011.

Polansky, Daniel. *The Vietnam War.* St. Louis, Mo.: Turtleback Books, 2013.

Ray, Michael (ed.). *Disco, Punk, New Wave, Heavy Metal, and More: Music in the 1970s and 1980s.* New York, N.Y.: Rosen Educational Service, 2012.

Scheeres, Julia. *A Thousand Lives: The Untold Story of Jonestown.* New York, N.Y.: Free Press, 2011.

Wittekind, Erika. *The United States v. Nixon.* Minneapolis, Minn.: Abdo Publishing Company, 2012.

Web Sites

archives.gov/exhibits/american_originals/nixon.html
The National Archives holds a wealth of information about this controversial time.

70ps.com/
The 70's Preservation Society features pop culture from the decade.

whitehouse.gov/history/presidents/jc39.html
The White House's offical fact page about Jimmy Carter.

Movies

Argo. Directed by Ben Affleck. Burbank, Calif.: Warner Bros. Entertainment, 2012.

This movie dramatizes the Iran Hostage Crisis.

Saturday Night Fever. Directed by John Badham. Hollywood, Calif.: Paramount Pictures, 1977.

A quintessential pop culture movie of the decade about the disco culture.

Index

Elliott, Cass, 29
Environmental Protection Agency (EPA), 83
Equal Rights Amendments (ERA), 54

F

feminism. *See* women's liberation movement.
Ford, Betty, 22
Ford, Gerald, 12, 53, 54
Foreman, George, 42
Franklin, Aretha, 30

G

Gates, Bill, 75
Gaye, Marvin, 30
Gladys Knight and the Pips, 30
Godfather, The, 24
Grateful Dead, 30
Grease, 26
Green, Al, 30

H

Haldeman, H. R., 53
Haley, Alex, 11
Hancock, Herbie, 30
Hendrix, Jimi, 29
Herrera, Omar Torrijos, 57
hippies, 8, 9
Hispanic Americans, 13
Holtzman, Elizabeth, 18
Humphrey, Hubert, 44

I

Iran, 66, 69

Israel, 7, 36, 39, 61, 62, 65, 66

J

Jaworski, Leon, 53
Jaws, 24, 26
Jobs, Steve, 73
Joel, Billy, 30
Johnson, Lyndon, 44, 47
Jones, Jim, 17
Jonestown, 8, 17, 84
Joplin, Janis, 29
Jordan, Barbara, 18

K

Kent State University, 47, 49
Khmer Rouge, 47
Khomeini, Ayatollah Ruhollah, 66
King, Billie Jean, 35, 36
Kissinger, Henry, 49
Klein, Calvin, 20
Knievel, Evel, 42

L

La Raza Unida, 13
Led Zeppelin, 30
Longest Walk, The, 14
Loren, Sophia, 22
Love Canal, 80, 83
Lucas, George, 26

M

Maharishi Mahesh Yogi, 14
Manilow, Barry, 30
Marley, Bob, 30
McGovern, George, 50
Mitchell, John, 53